Official Cambridge Exam Preparation

COMPACT

PRELIMINARY FOR SCHOOLS
SECOND EDITION

WITH AUDIO
DOWNLOAD

B1

WORKBOOK
WITHOUT ANSWERS

Laura Clyde

For the revised exam from 2020

Cambridge University Press

www.cambridge.org/elt

Cambridge Assessment English

www.cambridgeenglish.org

Information on this title: www.cambridge.org/9781108349109

© Cambridge University Press & Assessment and UCLES 2019

First published 2013
Second edition 2019

40 39 38 37 36 35 34 33 32 31 30 29 28 27 26 25 24 23 22 21

Printed in the Netherlands by Wilco BV

A catalogue record for this publication is available from the British Library

ISBN 978-1-108-34910-9 Workbook without answers with Audio Download

Contents

1 All about me!

Grammar

Present simple & present continuous

1 Complete these sentences with the present simple or present continuous of the verbs in brackets.

1 My school .... (organise) a ski trip to France every year.
2 My sister and I .... (stay) with our grandparents at the moment as our parents are on holiday.
3 I .... (try) to do all my homework on a Friday afternoon so I .... (not have) any at the weekend.
4 **A:** What .... you .... (do)?
   B: I .... (revise) for the exam tomorrow.
5 My mum usually .... (work) from home. She only .... (go) to the office when there is a meeting.
6 **A:** What language .... that man on the TV .... (speak)? Is it Spanish or Italian?
   B: Italian, I think.

-ing forms

2 Complete these sentences with the prepositions *about*, *at*, *in*, *of* or *to*.

1 Tony's good .... cooking – he makes delicious pizzas.
2 What school subject are you most interested ....?
3 I'm worried .... the exam tomorrow.
4 I'm looking forward .... the weekend.
5 She's not afraid .... anything!
6 I'm not very fond .... orange juice. I prefer apple juice.

3 Choose the correct verb forms to complete the conversation.

When I **(1)** *get / am getting* home from school, I hate **(2)** *start / starting* my homework straightaway. I like **(3)** *relax / relaxing* for a while and **(4)** *not do / not doing* anything! What about you?   2:34 ✓✓

I **(5)** *have / am having* drama club after school on Mondays, Wednesdays and Fridays. I don't mind **(6)** *be / being* so busy, but I often **(7)** *get / am getting* quite tired. So, on Tuesdays and Thursdays I enjoy **(8)** *not do / not doing* much at all. After I **(9)** *finish / am finishing* my homework, I love **(10)** *lie / lying* on the sofa listening to music.   2:37 ✓✓

Vocabulary

1 Look at these pictures. Write the correct letter next to each place.

1 canteen   ....   4 playground   ....   7 science lab   ....
2 classroom ....   5 school gym   ....   8 sports field ....
3 IT room   ....   6 school hall ....   9 tennis court ....

2 Complete these likes and dislikes about school with words from the box.

> a new sport   a school trip   a uniform
> an after-school club   classes   exams   good grades
> hard   homework   late   on stage   packed lunch

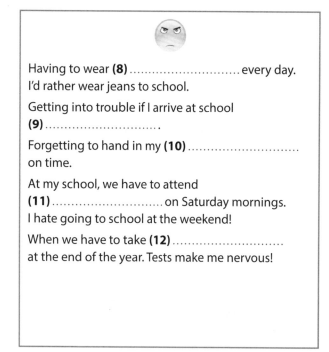

The chance to take up **(1)** .... – hockey in my case.

The chance to join **(2)** .... I go to chess, drama and cookery!

We go on **(3)** .... to a different place every term.

Getting **(4)** .... for my work – it doesn't happen very often, though!

Having a break from classes and eating my **(5)** ....

We perform **(6)** .... each year in our school play. It's great fun!

When I work really **(7)** .... in a lesson and feel I'm learning a lot.

Having to wear **(8)** .... every day. I'd rather wear jeans to school.

Getting into trouble if I arrive at school **(9)** ....

Forgetting to hand in my **(10)** .... on time.

At my school, we have to attend **(11)** .... on Saturday mornings. I hate going to school at the weekend!

When we have to take **(12)** .... at the end of the year. Tests make me nervous!

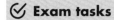 **Exam tasks**

Writing Part 1

Read this email from your friend Toby and the notes you have made.

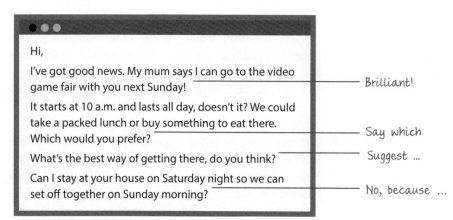

Hi,

I've got good news. My mum says I can go to the video game fair with you next Sunday! — Brilliant!

It starts at 10 a.m. and lasts all day, doesn't it? We could take a packed lunch or buy something to eat there. Which would you prefer? — Say which

What's the best way of getting there, do you think? — Suggest ...

Can I stay at your house on Saturday night so we can set off together on Sunday morning? — No, because ...

Write your email to Toby using all the notes.

Write your answer in about 100 words.

Reading Part 2

For each question, choose the correct answer.

The young people below all want to go to a camp this summer. Opposite there are descriptions of eight summer camps.

Decide which camp would be the most suitable for the people below.

1 Tim already knows how to cook, but he would like to improve his skills in the kitchen and learn how to make his own recipes. He'd also like the opportunity to meet a well-known chef.

2 Lucille loves ballet and acting and would like to improve her skills in both. Music is another of her interests and she can play the guitar and would like to learn the flute.

3 James is keen on football and supports a Spanish team. He doesn't speak any Spanish, but he is interested in learning it as fast as possible.

4 Penny's main interest is playing video games and she particularly likes ones that involve sport. She would like to learn how to create her own games.

5 Serena loves doing sport and is a very good swimmer. Her favourite subject at school is PE, but she also really enjoys biology and chemistry.

Summer camps

A If you like the idea of spending time at the beach while finding out more about the ocean, the Sealife summer camp is perfect for you. On this two-week camp, you will learn science about the sea. You'll also have plenty of opportunities to do water sports. Sign up now!

B Do you enjoy playing games on screens? Have you ever thought about designing one yourself? On this one-week camp, taught by the designer of the popular game *Tennis Tournament*, you will work with a partner to create a new video game. Sign up for this course and build the game you've always dreamed about!

C Are you interested in Spanish food and cooking, but don't know where to start? On this two-week camp for beginners, you will learn basic skills in the kitchen, as well as how to cook tasty dishes using fresh, healthy ingredients.

D On this four-week camp, you'll practise speaking and listening to Spanish from when you get up in the morning to when you go to bed at night. You'll have language classes, go on trips and practise playing football. You'll even get some tips from a star footballer. This camp is for beginner language students who want to improve quickly!

E Would you like to explore the world of movie-making by writing a screenplay, choosing the actors, directing, filming and acting? On this two-week camp, you'll spend the first week trying everything involved with making a film. In the second week, you choose a role and, in groups, make a film!

F For all young chefs out there, this is the course for you! Taught by qualified cookery teachers, you will spend a week learning how to make different dishes from all over the world, as well as inventing your own new ones. The course ends with a session given by the celebrity cook Margot McMar.

G Improve your Spanish and do sport at the same time on our two-week course by the sea. Taught by professional Spanish-speaking trainers, you will get the chance to play team sports such as volleyball, basketball, football and hockey, as well as individual sports like windsurfing and horse-riding.

H On this summer camp, you can improve your skills on a musical instrument, or learn how to play a new instrument of your choice, in one-to-one and group lessons with a professional musician. Drama classes are also offered, as well as classes in different types of dance.

Listening Part 2

🔊 02 For each question, choose the correct answer.

1 You will hear a girl trying to persuade her friend to join a school drama club. What does she say that convinces him to try it?
   A They are short of people.
   B He can do other things as well as acting.
   C He would be a good actor.

2 You will hear a girl talking to her brother about her new school uniform. What does she like about it?
   A the style of the jacket
   B the colour of the top
   C the design of the skirt

3 You will hear a boy telling his friend about a new teacher. Why does he prefer this teacher to his previous one?
   A He thinks she's a nicer person.
   B He understands things better in class.
   C He gets less homework now.

4 You will hear two classmates talking about a recent class project in which the girl got a high mark. What did the girl do that the boy did not do?
   A She used the internet for help.
   B She studied really hard.
   C She wrote things down.

5 You will hear two classmates talking about their school end-of-year trip. What do they disagree about?
   A the project they have to do
   B the places they are going to see
   C the food they will eat

6 You will hear a girl telling her friend about a summer camp she went on. How did she feel about it?
   A annoyed that she had to do so much sport
   B disappointed that she couldn't learn another language
   C unhappy that she had to share a tent

Reading Part 5

For each question, choose the correct answer.

The perfect school

Never needing to get up early, no uniform to wear, choosing what to study and when to study it. Is that the kind of school day that you (1) .... about? For children who are 'homeschooled', this is a (2) ....

Homeschooled children don't (3) .... school. Their parents teach them, or they do lessons in an online classroom with other homeschooled children. In the UK, nearly 30,000 children are homeschooled and in the USA about 1.5 million.

Homeschooling can be a good (4) .... for children who want to (5) .... on a subject that they are particularly good at, and spend less time on other subjects. It can also be helpful for children who have (6) .... problems at school. For example, they may have a learning difficulty, such as dyslexia.

	A		B		C		D	
1	A hope		B dream		C imagine		D wish	
2	A thought		B situation		C truth		D reality	
3	A attend		B appear		C arrive		D accompany	
4	A possibility		B benefit		C option		D tip	
5	A concentrate		B consider		C set		D fix	
6	A accepted		B received		C experienced		D involved	

2 Winning & losing

Grammar

Past simple & past continuous

1 Complete these sentences with the past simple of the verbs.

1 He .... (buy) a very expensive pair of trainers last week.
2 When .... you .... (learn) to play tennis?
3 They .... (not be) very happy with the result.
4 My school .... (organise) a fantastic sports day last year.
5 She .... (become) an Olympic skiing champion in 2018.
6 .... (be) he upset about losing the match?
7 I .... (not take part) in the competition because I .... (be) injured.
8 We .... (do) really well this year in basketball – we .... (win) the school championship!

2 Complete this text with the past continuous of the verbs in the box.

> eat   laugh   shine
> sit   sunbathe   talk

This time last week I **(1)** .... outside in a comfortable chair at a restaurant by the beach having lunch with my family. We **(2)** .... a delicious rice dish called 'paella'. The sun **(3)** .... and people **(4)** .... and swimming in the sea. I **(5)** .... to my cousin Alex and we **(6)** .... a lot. It was fun!

3 Choose the correct verb forms to complete this text.

It **(1)** *was / was being* the last two minutes of the match and we **(2)** *lost / were losing* 2-1. I **(3)** *had / was having* the ball and I **(4)** *saw / was seeing* a chance to score, but while I **(5)** *ran / was running* towards the goal, I **(6)** *slipped / was slipping* and **(7)** *fell over / was falling over*. We **(8)** *didn't win / weren't winning* the match, which was a shame!

Vocabulary

1 Match the sentence beginnings (1–6) with the correct endings (a–f).

1 Don't give in –   a my application form for the tennis club.
2 He's staying in   b to the game as all the tickets were sold out.
3 I believe in   c tonight – he's too tired to go out.
4 Don't you want to join in d with the game?
5 I forgot to hand in   e you could still win the game!
6 We couldn't get in   f my team – I know we can win!

2 Complete these sentences with the correct form of the words in the box.

> achieve   beat   defeat   lose   succeed   win

1 She played really well but didn't manage to .... her opponent.
2 Our team hasn't .... a match yet this season. I don't know what we're doing wrong.
3 He got to the semi-final, but was .... there by a much younger player.
4 They have played well all season and have .... in staying at the top of the league.
5 We .... the match when the other team scored a goal in the last few seconds of the game.
6 Millions of teenagers would like to become famous footballers, but only a tiny number .... their dream.

3 Complete this text with words in the box.

> athletic   athletics   competition   competitive

I don't consider myself to be a very **(1)** .... person, but I'm not bad at sports that involve running, jumping and throwing – in other words, **(2)** .... At my school every summer, we hold a sports day, which is actually a big **(3)** .... where we compete against other schools. I'm not usually a very **(4)** .... person – normally, I don't care whether I win or lose – but at the sports day I really try and do my best to win!

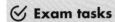
Reading Part 4

Five sentences have been removed from the text below.

For each question, choose the correct answer.

There are three extra sentences which you do not need to use.

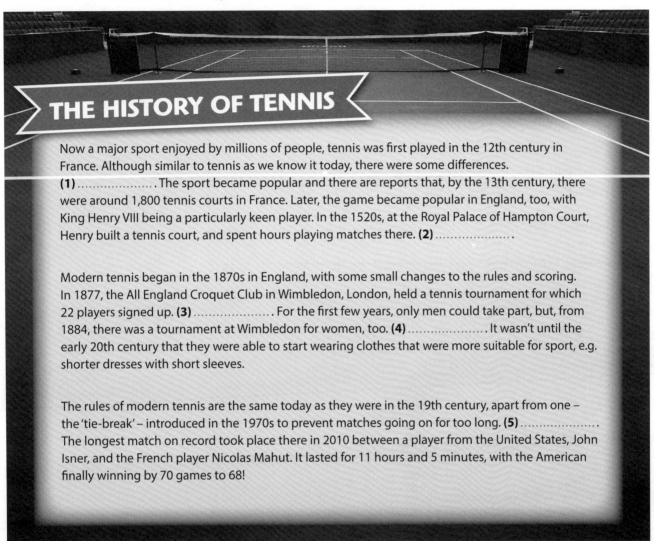

THE HISTORY OF TENNIS

Now a major sport enjoyed by millions of people, tennis was first played in the 12th century in France. Although similar to tennis as we know it today, there were some differences. **(1)** .... The sport became popular and there are reports that, by the 13th century, there were around 1,800 tennis courts in France. Later, the game became popular in England, too, with King Henry VIII being a particularly keen player. In the 1520s, at the Royal Palace of Hampton Court, Henry built a tennis court, and spent hours playing matches there. **(2)** ....

Modern tennis began in the 1870s in England, with some small changes to the rules and scoring. In 1877, the All England Croquet Club in Wimbledon, London, held a tennis tournament for which 22 players signed up. **(3)** .... For the first few years, only men could take part, but, from 1884, there was a tournament at Wimbledon for women, too. **(4)** .... It wasn't until the early 20th century that they were able to start wearing clothes that were more suitable for sport, e.g. shorter dresses with short sleeves.

The rules of modern tennis are the same today as they were in the 19th century, apart from one – the 'tie-break' – introduced in the 1970s to prevent matches going on for too long. **(5)** .... The longest match on record took place there in 2010 between a player from the United States, John Isner, and the French player Nicolas Mahut. It lasted for 11 hours and 5 minutes, with the American finally winning by 70 games to 68!

A This was the first of the tennis championships at this location.

B They had to play wearing long dresses with long sleeves, and hats.

C Successful players made lots of money from tennis even in the 1800s.

D In fact, that court still exists today.

E However, at Wimbledon, this rule doesn't apply.

F Tennis became popular in the USA, too, although with different rules.

G At the Wimbledon tennis championship, players still have to wear white clothes.

H You played with your hand, not a racket, for example.

Listening Part 3

🔊 03 For each question, write the correct answer in the gap.

Write **one** or **two** words or a **number** or a **date** or a **time**.

You will hear a woman called Susan Chapman telling a group of secondary school pupils about a sports centre.

Westfield Sports Centre

The Centre was closed for improvements until **(1)** .... of this year.

New facilities and activities include:

An **(2)** .... swimming pool

Team sport: **(3)** ....

Individual sport: a **(4)** .... class

Two new **(5)** .... courts

Fees: Under 18s pay **(6)** .... less than usual for membership at the moment.

Reading Part 5

For each question, choose the correct answer.

ORGANISED SPORT

Lots of people love organised sport, whether a team game or an individual activity. They enjoy being a member of a team or a club so they have the opportunity to **(1)** .... part in matches and events. As well, they enjoy sharing the **(2)** ...., or failure, with others.

However, there are many people who just don't like organised sport and who have to find other ways to **(3)** .... fit and healthy. Perhaps they had a bad experience with a **(4)** .... sport when they were younger. Maybe they feel embarrassed because they think they're not very good at a sport and worry about disappointing the rest of the team if they **(5)** .... badly. Organised sports are usually all about competitions and **(6)** ...., and for some people, this pressure is too stressful.

1	**A** join	**B** give	**C** take	**D** make
2	**A** success	**B** score	**C** effort	**D** result
3	**A** continue	**B** reach	**C** bring	**D** keep
4	**A** limited	**B** separate	**C** particular	**D** general
5	**A** achieve	**B** perform	**C** produce	**D** deliver
6	**A** challenging	**B** staying	**C** reaching	**D** winning

Writing Part 2

Your English teacher has asked you to write a story.

Your story must begin with this sentence:

This was the most important game of the season and we were losing.

Write your **story** in about **100 words**.

3 Let's shop!

Grammar

Order of adjectives

1 Reorder the words in bold to complete the sentences. Then match the sentences to the comments.

1 I love your **black / boots / new / leather**!

....

2 I've only got this **old / cotton / jacket / cheap**.

....

3 Look at that **shirt / red / beautiful / silk**!

....

4 He usually wears **wool / grey / old-fashioned / jumpers**.

....

5 She's wearing some **interesting / earrings / silver / big**.

....

6 My grandmother gave me a **pale / bracelet / gold / valuable**.

....

a He really needs to change his look.

b I need something warmer and smarter.

c I'm not sure if I like them or not.

d It was so kind of her.

e The colour would look fantastic on you!

f Where did you buy them?

Comparative & superlative adjectives

2 Complete this conversation with the comparative or superlative form of the adjectives in brackets. Add extra words where necessary.

A: So which top do you think is **(1)** .... (good), the blue or the brown one?

B: Well, the blue one is £19.99 and the brown one is £24.99, so the blue one is **(2)** .... (cheap). And it looks **(3)** .... (comfortable) the brown one.

A: That's true, but brown is a **(4)** .... (fashionable) colour, don't you think?

B: Maybe, but for me, comfort and price are the **(5)** .... (important) things to think about.

A: You're **(6)** .... (bad) my mum!

B: No, I'm just **(7)** .... (sensible) you! I know, why don't we go and look in Grant's. It's **(8)** .... (big) this shop. And it's usually **(9)** .... (expensive).

A: Yes, they have the **(10)** .... (good) prices in town. Let's go there.

Pronouns

3 Complete these sentences with *who*, *which* or *where*.

1 We had some lovely ice cream at that new café, ... is also famous for its delicious chocolate cake.

2 That's the shop .... they sell the best shoes in town.

3 He's the boy .... designs clothes.

4 There's a new game shop in town .... you can play the games before you buy them.

5 Do you know anyone .... doesn't like shopping?

6 I bought the trousers from an online company .... makes clothes from recycled material.

Vocabulary

1 Label these pictures with words in the box.

> bracelet collar dress earring gloves heel
> jacket jeans jumper necklace sandals shirt
> skirt sleeve sweatshirt T-shirt top trainers

1 ....
2 ....
3 ....
4 ....
5 ....
6 ....
7 ....
8 ....
9 ....
10 ....
11 ....
12 ....
13 ....
14 ....
15 ....
16 ....
17 ....
18 ....

2 For each question, choose the correct answer.

1 What is the best material for a winter coat?
   A cotton   B wool   C silk
2 What is a wedding ring usually made from?
   A plastic   B silver   C gold
3 What is the most suitable material for a shirt to wear in hot weather?
   A fur   B cotton   C leather
4 Which of these is a thin, smooth material often used to make clothes for special occasions?
   A silver   B leather   C silk
5 Which of these is made from the skin of animals and is used to make shoes and bags?
   A fur   B leather   C plastic
6 Which of these materials is man-made?
   A plastic   B silver   C wool
7 Which of these materials is a grey-white colour and used to make coins and jewellery?
   A silver   B gold   C plastic

3 Circle the odd word out in each group.

1 comfortable casual pink smart stylish
2 department store market traditional second-hand shop online
3 purple cream dark green light blue casual
4 skirt jumper sweatshirt jacket

Listening Part 4

🔊 **04** For each question, choose the correct answer.

You will hear an interview with teenager Ella McHugh, who runs a business designing and making special products.

1 What gave Ella the idea for her business?
   A She was looking for a way of using old objects she had at home.
   B She wanted to help people who don't have electric power.
   C She heard about a project that she thought was really good.
2 What did people think of Ella's first products?
   A They liked one of the products and suggested that she make more to sell.
   B They were enthusiastic about both of the products.
   C They wanted her to sell some more old clothes.
3 Ella considers that her business started when she
   A first sold some products.
   B started offering products on the internet.
   C began producing products.
4 Ella now has help with the business because
   A the amount of work was more than she could do.
   B two of her friends asked to be part of it.
   C she needed a manager.
5 What does Ella particularly like about working with her friends?
   A They can help her when she's feeling stressed.
   B They can help her think up ideas for new products.
   C They have the responsibility for creating new items.
6 Ella says her parents think that
   A she isn't doing as well at school as before.
   B she doesn't have enough time for school work.
   C she's learning things that aren't taught at school.

Reading Part 5

For each question, choose the correct answer.

LIVING WITHOUT MONEY

Do we really need money? Or could we organise our lives so that we can **(1)** .... using it? Some people are trying to do just that by joining 'bartering' communities, where they **(2)** .... goods, such as food, clothes, books and games, or services, like babysitting or transport, without using money. This could involve a direct trade – so a video game for a video game, a book for a book. Another alternative is to pay by using credit. For example, you would get different goods or services in return for the ones you **(3)** ....

Of course, people have swapped and shared things for centuries, but nowadays with the internet, the **(4)** .... to give and receive things without using money is no longer limited to your **(5)** .... area as it was in the past. Through websites and apps, you can **(6)** .... anywhere in the world for people who want what you have to offer and have something that you want in return.

1 A prevent   B avoid   C refuse   D discount
2 A exchange   B turn   C deal   D switch
3 A present   B afford   C provide   D apply
4 A occasion   B opportunity   C power   D variety
5 A common   B local   C neighbourhood D public
6 A see   B study   C solve   D search

Reading Part 1

For each question, choose the correct answer.

1

> **SOUTHERN TRAINS**
> **TICKETS AND RAILPASSES**
> **on sale here**
>
> *OUT OF ORDER*
> *Please use machine*
> *on platform*

A You cannot buy train tickets today.
B You must buy train tickets from a different place.
C You have to order tickets in advance.

2

> **TREND FASHION**
> ## CHANGING ROOMS
> **Up to five items only are permitted at a time.**

A You cannot take more than five things into the changing rooms.
B You cannot take five things into the changing rooms at the same time.
C You cannot spend a long time trying things on in the changing rooms.

3

> Mum, I'm having problems with my maths homework. Can you help when you get home from work? I know you get back late tonight, but that doesn't matter. Love, Jake
>
> Monday 15:01

A Jake is trying to persuade his mother to come home early from work.
B Jake is asking for his mother's help and doesn't mind when this is.
C Jake wants his mother to confirm that she has to work late tonight.

4

> **WIN A TRIP TO LONDON FASHION WEEK!**
>
> **Design competition**
> *Only entries from people under 16 will be accepted.*

A The winning design will appear at London Fashion Week.
B Only 16-year-olds can enter the competition.
C There is a maximum age limit for this competition.

5

> **From:** jjones@hatsteadhigh.co.uk
> **To:** Parents
> **Subject:** School sweatshirts
>
> Dear all,
> Parents who wish to order a sweatshirt for their son or daughter should inform me by email by 18th May, stating which size you require.
> Regards,
> Jane Jones

A To get a sweatshirt, students must tell the school their size before 18th May.
B All parents have to buy a school sweatshirt for their child by 18thMay.
C Parents who want a sweatshirt for their child should tell the school by 18th May.

Writing Part 2

You see this notice in an international student magazine.

> Articles wanted!
> ### MONEY
> How do young people in your country get money, e.g. from part-time jobs, parents?
> What kind of things do you spend your money on?
> How important is it to save money?
> Tell us what you think!
> Write an article answering these questions and we will publish the most interesting articles in our magazine.

Write your article in about 100 words.

Grammar

Present perfect

1 Complete these sentences with the present perfect of the verb in brackets.

1 Can I call you back? I .... just
.... (wake up).
2 I............................... (live) in this town all of my life.
3 **A:** Is Ellie there?
B: No, sorry, she .... (go) out.
4 I............................... (not finish) my homework, so I can't go to football practice today.
5 She .... (play) three video games this morning and it's still only 10 o'clock!
6 .... you .... (see) that new film?
7 They .... (not decide) what to buy her for her birthday.
8 We .... (play) in ten different countries on this tour.

2 Choose the correct word to complete these sentences.

1 I haven't read that book *yet / already*. I'm going to start it at the weekend.
2 Have we *just / already* arrived? That was really quick.
3 I've been at this school *for / since* last year.
4 He hasn't seen his grandfather *for / since* a year now.
5 She's *just / yet* phoned now. She's on her way.
6 We're not too late – the film has *just / already* started.
7 I've been a fan of hers *for / since* at least five years.
8 It hasn't rained *for / since* April.

3 Exam candidates often make mistakes with the present perfect. Correct the mistakes in these sentences.

1 I saw a lot of interesting things here in Paris.
....
2 We live in Bangladesh for two years.
....
3 I am not using my bike and I decide to sell it.
....
4 I need a laptop now I moved to a smaller house.
....
5 Dear Wendy, I receive your letter.
....
6 I think it's a beautiful place because I've visited it two years ago.
....
7 I don't need it because I have buy a new car.
....
8 You know I want one for a long time.
....

Vocabulary

1 Choose the correct adjective to complete these sentences.

1 Their new song is *amazing / amazed*. I love it.
2 My brother hates horror films. He gets really *frightening / frightened*.
3 She was *disappointing / disappointed* that she didn't get a part in the film.
4 Are you *interested / interesting* in learning a musical instrument?
5 We weren't *surprised / surprising* about her winning the talent competition. She sings really well.
6 I'm so *excited / exciting*! A story I wrote is going to be published in an online magazine!
7 It's really *annoyed / annoying* when you're watching something online and it suddenly stops.
8 You look *worried / worrying*. What's the matter?

2 Complete these sentences with the correct preposition in the box.

about	by	of	with

1 I'm really excited .... the holiday.
2 What are you worried .... ?
3 She was impressed .... the special effects.
4 I'm not afraid .... anything!
5 It's normal to be anxious .... exams.
6 I wasn't satisfied .... my performance at the concert.
7 He's serious .... wanting to be an actor when he's older.
8 My brother's annoyed .... me because I lost his headphones.
9 I'm jealous .... your new bike – I want one like that, too!

3 Complete this text with *take part*, *take place* and *take up* in the correct form.

When my grandmother retired two years ago, she decided to
(1) .... the flute – at the age of 67! She has learnt a lot since then and now plays pretty well. She has even **(2)** .... in a concert with other musicians.
It **(3)** .... in a big concert hall in our town and hundreds of people came to it.

✓ **Exam tasks**

Reading Part 4

Five sentences have been removed from the text below.

For each question, choose the correct answer.

There are three extra sentences which you do not need to use.

The secret rock star

I've always known that my mum loves music and is very musical. She can play several instruments, including the guitar and the violin. She is actually really amazing on the guitar.
(1) .... And she is always singing around the house.

I didn't know until recently, though, that, back in the 1990s, my mum played in a pretty famous band. **(2)** .... He mentioned a video he had seen on YouTube of a '90s band playing live. He thought one of the singers looked like my mum and sent me the link to the video. I could see the similarity, but the woman's hairstyle and clothes were completely different to my mum's and she looked so young.

I wanted to know for certain, so I showed my mum the video to see how she would react. **(3)** .... It was my mum. But why had she never told me about it?

(4) .... At the beginning, she loved it. But, after a few years, it wasn't fun anymore: playing concerts in a different city every night, spending 24 hours a day with the other members of the band. She decided to give it up and teach the guitar instead.

(5) .... But that was then. Nowadays, I think to myself, 'My mum, a former rock star!' – that's so cool!

A When I mentioned this, I could see that he was surprised.
B As soon as it started to play, I could see from her face that Jake was right.
C I wish he'd warned me about what it showed.
D In fact, they had played all over the world and made lots of money.
E I found this out about a month ago through a friend of mine, Jake.
F In fact, she teaches it to private students who come to our house for classes.
G After finally hearing her story, I was still a little annoyed that she had kept her past a secret.
H She explained that it was a period of her life that she wanted to forget.

Reading Part 6

For each question, write the correct answer.

Write one word for each gap.

The winner of the Young Film-maker of the Year contest shares some tips about film-making on his blog

Firstly, you don't need a lot of expensive equipment **(1)** .... make a film. If you can't afford a video camera, then use your smartphone.

A great way to learn is by watching lots **(2)** .... films. Study the characters, the acting, how the camera is used, and copy the techniques you think are the **(3)** .... successful.

I recommend keeping your initial film-making projects simple so use what you've got around you – your home, your street and your friends. Also, begin with short films. A good story can **(4)** .... told in just a few minutes.

Get advice and ideas from people **(5)** .... opinion you respect, but at the same time trust yourself and make the film that you want.

Finally, make sure people know about your film. Easy ways to do this include posting **(6)** .... social media and looking for young film-maker competitions to enter!

Writing Part 2

Your English teacher has asked you to write a story.
Your story must begin with this sentence:

She and the other competitors were waiting to hear the result of the film competition.

Write your **story** in about **100 words**.

Listening Part 1

🔊 05 For each question, choose the correct answer.

1 How is the girl going to celebrate her birthday?

2 How old was the man when he started making films?

A  B  C

3 Which instrument does the girl still play?

A  B  C

4 Who won the young film-maker competition?

A  B  C

5 When do the girls decide to go to the concert?

A  B  C

6 What did the woman buy her niece for her birthday?

A  B  C

7 What time do the boys need to leave for the cinema?

A 17:00 B 17:15 C 18:00

Extreme diets

Grammar

Future forms

1 Choose the best future verb forms to complete these dialogues.

1

Girl: What **(1)** *are we having / do we have* for lunch, Dad? It smells really good.

Father: Soup. It **(2)** *is / will be* ready in 15 minutes.

Girl: OK, but I'm really hungry, so I think I **(3)** *'ll have / 'm having* an apple while I'm waiting.

2

Granny: What time **(4)** *does / will* your football training finish on Mondays?

Boy: It's 6 p.m., but tonight we **(5)** *'re finishing / will finish* at a quarter to six because they need the pitch for a match.

3

Jane: I **(6)** *go / 'm going* shopping on Saturday afternoon. I want to spend my birthday money. Do you want to come with me?

Maria: I'd love to, but I **(7)** *'m going to be / 'm being* too busy.

Jane: Really? Why?

Maria: I **(8)** *'m having / have* six exams next week and I know I **(9)** *won't pass / 'm not passing* them unless I do a lot of work. So, I **(10)** *'ll get / 'm going to get* up early on Saturday morning and revise all weekend.

2 Complete these sentences with a word or phrase in the box.

'll x2   are you going to   're going to   's going to
's having   isn't going to   will   won't

1 We .... order a pizza and watch a film tonight. I already know what type of pizza I want!

2 She .... win the competition, I'm sure. Her entry is definitely the best.

3 That looks difficult. I .... help you if you like.

4 Jan called me to tell me that she .... a party on Saturday evening. She's already bought the food and drink for it.

5 .... you have time to go and buy some milk, do you think?

6 We probably .... use petrol in the future as a fuel for vehicles. We .... use cleaner fuels.

7 Jamie .... come round this evening in the end. He's ill.

8 What .... do this weekend? Have you got plans yet?

3 Complete these sentences with a future form of the verbs in brackets.

1 I .... (train) to be a chef when I leave school. It's always been my ambition.

2 I'm sure that sooner or later the government .... (stop) so much plastic being used.

3 They .... (not go) on holiday this year. They can't afford it.

4 What .... you .... (do) to celebrate your birthday this year?

5 Look at that little boy running by the swimming pool. He .... (fall in)!

6 The flight .... (leave) at 8 o'clock this evening.

Vocabulary

1 Circle the odd word out in each group.

1 peach corn grape pineapple strawberry
2 cabbage cod salmon tuna
3 beef lamb lettuce turkey
4 corn chicken carrot spinach lettuce

2 Complete these definitions with a word in the box.

> boiled   fried   frozen   raw

1 Food that is uncooked is ....
2 When food is kept at a very low temperature it is
....
3 When food is cooked in oil it is ....
4 When food is cooked in very hot water it is
....

3 Complete these sentences with the prepositions
away, *down*, *off*, *on*, *out* or *up*.

1 This room's such a mess. Can you help me put things
.... ?
2 They've put the price of mobile phone calls
.... from 2p to 5p per minute.
3 I've put .... 2 kilos over the summer
holidays – I think it's because I've not had PE.
4 She's putting .... her birthday party until
next weekend because she's ill.
5 Listen, everyone, you're not allowed to put your
mobile phone .... in class, OK?
6 Remember to put the candles .... before
you go to bed, won't you?
7 I've just realised, I forgot to put my bracelet back
.... after my swimming class.
8 The course is full at the moment, but I've put my
name .... on the waiting list for a place.

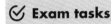

Exam tasks

Reading Part 6

For each question, write the correct answer.

Write one word for each gap.

Changing my diet

Two years ago, I found out that certain foods were making me ill. This was a big shock, as it meant that I had to stop eating things that I loved, such **(1)** .... bread, pizza and ice cream. Once I changed my diet, I felt so much better because I didn't have stomach ache or feel tired **(2)** .... the time. However, I found having to eat **(3)** .... same dishes made from foods that didn't upset my stomach pretty boring. So I started to research other things that I could eat, and this is how I became really interested **(4)** .... food and started inventing my own recipes. A friend suggested that I should start a blog about my experience, and include my recipes, along **(5)** .... photos of the dishes I prepare, so I did that. And now it **(6)** .... become a really popular food blog. Amazingly, I now have nearly 10,000 people reading my blog posts!

Reading Part 1

For each question, choose the correct answer.

1

This label is advising people about

A when to open the soup.
B how to cook the soup.
C how long the soup lasts.

2

HILL'S SCHOOL

**Packed lunches are to be eaten
in the canteen**

**It is forbidden to eat
in the classroom**

This notice is telling pupils

A why they must bring a packed lunch to school.
B where they must eat lunch at school.
C when they must go to the canteen for lunch.

3

**Treat your park
like your home**

**Use the rubbish
bins provided**

Keep your town tidy

What is this notice encouraging people to do?

A to take part in a new recycling project
B to spend more time at their local park
C to put garbage in locations provided by the park

4

Kate, our 'food health' project is due in next Friday, as you know. We need to start working on it immediately, otherwise we won't get it finished in time. I'm free all day tomorrow. Suzy

Tuesday 2:34

A Suzy is warning Kate about what will happen if they don't do something soon.
B Suzy is asking for some information that Kate hasn't provided yet.
C Suzy is advising Kate about how to do a school project.

5

Choose from a range of delicious dishes from the menu

*Or why not
ask your waiter about*
NEW *daily specials?*

What is the purpose of this notice?

A to tell customers about the kind of the food that the restaurant offers
B to suggest that customers enquire about the choices that are available each day
C to inform customers that the chef is available to prepare special orders on request

Listening Part 3

🔊 06 For each question, write the correct answer in the gap.

Write one or two words or a number or date or a time.

You will hear a teacher giving her students some information about a class trip to a farm.

Before we get there

bus goes at **(1)** ....

a good idea to take some **(2)** ....

At the farm

feed the **(3)** .... at the farm

pick some **(4)** .... to take home

try the **(5)** .... there

Information about the farm

check website at

(6) www. ....com

Writing Part 1

Read the email from your English-speaking friend Ana and the notes you have made.

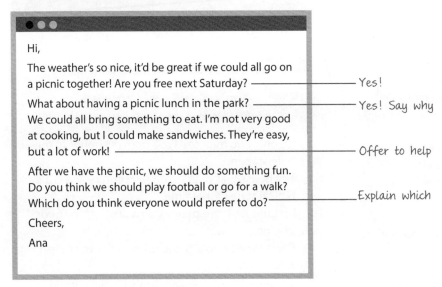

Hi,

The weather's so nice, it'd be great if we could all go on a picnic together! Are you free next Saturday? ——— Yes!

What about having a picnic lunch in the park? ——— Yes! Say why
We could all bring something to eat. I'm not very good at cooking, but I could make sandwiches. They're easy, but a lot of work! ——— Offer to help

After we have the picnic, we should do something fun. Do you think we should play football or go for a walk? Which do you think everyone would prefer to do? ——— Explain which

Cheers,

Ana

Write your email to Ana using all the notes.

Write your answer in about 100 words.

My home

Grammar

used to

1 Complete these sentences with the correct form of *used to* and a verb in the box.

be	go	not get	have	not let	not like	play

1 My father .... tennis every weekend, but now he only plays once a month.
2 I .... coffee when I was younger, but now I love it.
3 There .... a cinema in my town, but now it's a fast-food restaurant.
4 .... you .... long hair when you were younger or has it always been short?
5 My parents .... me play video games, but now they can't stop me!
6 I'm sure that winters .... so cold. I think the climate has changed.
7 Where .... you .... on holiday when you were a child, Mum?

Verbs followed by infinitive / -ing form

2 Choose the correct verb forms to complete these sentences.
1 We promised *to keep / keeping* in touch.
2 He's learning *to play / playing* the guitar.
3 They're teaching me *to play / playing* tennis.
4 I don't miss *to get up / getting up* early every day.
5 She always does her homework on Fridays, to avoid *to do / doing* it at the weekend.
6 They suggested *going / to go* for a pizza tomorrow.
7 I can't imagine *to live / living* anywhere else.

do, make, have, go

3 Complete these sentences with the correct form of *do*, *make*, *go* or *have*.

1 She .... well in the competition last week.
2 My parents are .... away next weekend to celebrate their wedding anniversary.
3 He always takes ages to .... up his mind.
4 Let's .... a party on Saturday.
5 How often do you .... shopping?
6 I always .... the washing up after lunch.
7 What time do you usually .... lunch?

Vocabulary

1 Look at these pictures. Complete the words.

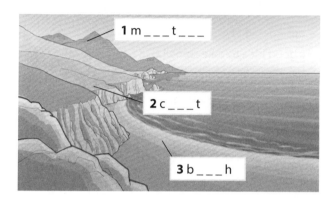

1 m _ _ _ t _ _ _
2 c _ _ _ t
3 b _ _ _ h

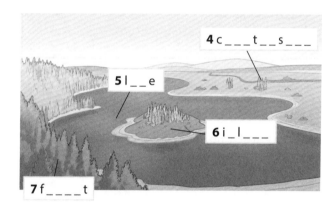

4 c _ _ _ t _ _ s _ _ _
5 l _ _ e
6 i _ l _ _ _
7 f _ _ _ _ t

2 Match words in the box with these sentences.

convenient	cosy	crowded
huge	lively	peaceful	traditional

1 It's only two minutes' walk from my house to the train station. ....
2 The house was built in the 19th century and is a typical style of that time. ....
3 Isn't this nice? No people, no noise, just the birds singing. ....
4 There's always lots going on in my town at the weekends. ....
5 It's snowing outside, but inside it's so nice and warm. ....
6 Their new house is really big – it's got five bedrooms and four bathrooms! ....
7 My dad doesn't like going to places in the city where there are lots of people. ....

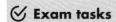

Reading Part 3

For each question, choose the correct answer.

Student Adam Brown talks about growing up in a tiny house

I was nine when my parents first had the idea of moving from a normal-sized flat in the city to a small place in the countryside, and I was eleven by the time we actually did it. And when I say small, I mean really, really small. Our new home was about the size of a typical garage. Compared to the car-park-sized flat where we used to live, it was tiny.

We built our tiny house ourselves on a piece of land about two hours' drive from the city. We used to go there every weekend and during holidays to work on it, but, even so, it took nearly two years to finish. My mum designed the house to include all the basic things that a normal house has but fitted into a much smaller space. My 'bedroom' was built in a space under the roof that I could reach by ladder.

My parents were very happy with our new life. They enjoyed being able to grow our own fruit and vegetables and keep chickens to provide us with eggs. They were particularly pleased about not having to pay for power and fuel because we could produce our own electricity from the sun. We also collected wood from the land around us to burn for heat.

I remember that it took me a few months to get used to living in such a small space. At first, I missed having all my favourite toys and books around me. Before we moved from the city, we had had to give away most of our things because there wasn't enough room for them anymore, but now I don't mind having fewer things. And one thing I love about our tiny home is being able to spend so much more time outside – something I didn't do in the city very often. And I do a lot more things with my parents, which is great.

I'm away at university now, and share a flat with other students, where my bedroom is about the same size as my whole family home! When I go back to see my parents, I find it hard to manage now in such a small space. I don't think I'll choose 'tiny living' for myself in the future, but I'm glad that I've had the experience of it.

---

1 Why does Adam compare his old and new homes in the first paragraph?
A to say that living in different homes is normal for him
B to discuss the advantages of living in a small home
C to make it clear how small his new home is
D to suggest that flats are better than houses

2 What is Adam doing in the second paragraph?
A complaining about how the house was designed
B giving information about the building and design of the house
C warning about the difficulties of building a small house
D explaining why his mum wanted to build a small house

3 What did Adam's parents like most about their new home?
A They could enjoy the land around them.
B They could easily get the wood they needed.
C They could keep animals.
D They could get essential things for free.

4 In the fourth paragraph, how does Adam feel about living in a tiny home?
A He has grown to like his new home over time.
B He dislikes not having enough room for his things.
C He wishes he had more time to be alone at his home.
D He is getting used to spending so much time outdoors.

5 What might Adam write now in his diary about living in a tiny home?
A I wish I hadn't had to spend so many years living in a tiny home.
B I'm not that keen on tiny living now I'm older, but I'm happy that I've done it.
C Why did Mum and Dad ever want to build a tiny home and move from the city?
D As soon as I get the chance, I'm going to build my own tiny home to live in.

Reading Part 5

For each question, choose the correct answer.

THE ALHAMBRA

I recently visited the Alhambra palace in southern Spain. I **(1)** .... it to be the most beautiful palace in the world. Other people must share my **(2)** .... as it is the most visited historic monument in Spain. In fact, it **(3)** .... three million visitors every year.

The Alhambra is located on a hill above the city of Granada and, **(4)** .... of many magnificent buildings, as well as courtyards and gardens. The place was first built in the 13th century by the Moorish king of the time, Mohammed I. The king paid special attention to the **(5)** .... of the palace. In particular, every single wall in all of the buildings are **(6)** .... with beautiful patterns which visitors can still admire today.

1	**A** consider	**B** feel	**C** understand	**D** accept
2	**A** thought	**B** hope	**C** opinion	**D** suggestion
3	**A** interests	**B** produces	**C** attracts	**D** brings
4	**A** includes	**B** involves	**C** exists	**D** consists
5	**A** design	**B** type	**C** model	**D** version
6	**A** dressed	**B** drawn	**C** decorated	**D** displayed

Writing Part 2

Your English teacher has asked you to write a story. Your story must begin with this sentence:

When I looked out of the window, I couldn't believe it.

Write your **story** in about **100 words**.

Listening Part 1

🔊 **07** For each question, choose the correct answer.

1 Where is Elena moving to?

2 What job is the boy's mother doing now?

3 Where is the girl now?

  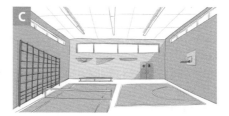

4 What will the weather be like in the north today?

5 What does Sally still need for her room?

6 Which was the last place they visited on the school trip?

7 Where did the boy stay on holiday?

7 In the wild

Grammar

Past perfect

1 Complete this text with the past simple or past perfect of the verbs in brackets.

Last week, I **(1)** .... (go) to our local zoo with my grandmother. She **(2)** .... (tell) me that it was the first time that she **(3)** .... (be) there since she was a young girl and it was interesting to hear from her how much the place **(4)** .... (change). Back then, she **(5)** .... (say), animals like lions and tigers weren't kept in the same conditions as they are today, with big spaces to move around in. They **(6)** .... (spend) most of their time in small cages and looked pretty bored and unhappy. In fact, seeing the animals like that was the reason why she **(7)** .... (not want) to go to the zoo again until recently, after I **(8)** .... (tell) her about another time that I **(9)** .... (be) to the zoo and what I **(10)** .... (see).

Reported speech

2 Complete these reported speech sentences.

1 'I haven't seen the baby lion,' the boy said.
The boy said he .... the baby lion.
2 'I'm really enjoying the trip,' Maria said.
Maria said she .... really ....
the trip.
3 'We will go to the butterfly exhibition next week,'
Mum said.
Mum said we .... to the butterfly
exhibition the following week.
4 'Do you want a piece of cake?' Dad asked.
Dad asked me if I .... a piece of
cake.
5 'Have you finished your homework?' my friend
asked me.
My friend asked me whether I ....
my homework.
6 'Pick up that litter you just dropped!' the park
keeper told the boy.
The park keeper told the boy ....
the litter he .... just ....
7 'Don't be late tomorrow,' the teacher told us.
The teacher told us .... late the
next day.
8 'You should go on the trip,' my friend said to me.
My friend persuaded me .... on
the trip.

Vocabulary

1 Match definitions (1–10) with the correct animal (a–j).

1 a very large, grey animal with big ears and a very long nose
2 a big animal with black hair, like a large monkey
3 a large animal that lives in the desert and that can manage without water for months
4 a small, black animal, like a mouse, that flies at night
5 a large, black and white sea bird that swims but cannot fly
6 a large fish with very sharp teeth
7 a small creature with eight long legs which catches insects in a web
8 a very large animal that looks like a large fish, lives in the sea, and breathes air through a hole at the top of its head
9 a colourful bird that can copy what people say
10 a long, thin creature with no legs

a bat
b camel
c elephant
d gorilla
e parrot
f penguin
g shark
h snake
i spider
j whale

2 Match the words in the box to the pictures.

> desert   ice   jungle   ocean   river
> sunset   waterfall

1 ....

2 ....

3 ....

4 ....

5 ....

6 ....

7 ....

3 Choose the correct word to complete these sentences.

1 There are no clouds. The sky is completely *rare / clear*.
2 It can get very hot and *humid / freezing* in places by the sea in summer.
3 These birds are very *rare / cruel* nowadays – there are only a few left in the world.
4 It is so cold that the river has *frozen / calm*.
5 There's no wind and the sea is *calm / freezing* – hardly a wave.

4 Complete this text with words in the box.

> climate change   litter   oil   pollution   protect

What can you and your family do to help **(1)** .... the environment?

• Don't drop **(2)** .... on the street! Put your rubbish in a bin.

• Get an electric car. This will help cause less air **(3)** ....

• Don't use **(4)** .... as a fuel in your home. Use power made by the sun or the wind instead.

The world is getting hotter. **(5)** .... is really happening. Believe it and help stop it!

✓ **Exam tasks**

Listening Part 4

🔊 08   For each question, choose the correct answer.

You will hear an interview with a young man called Rick who is working as a volunteer at an animal rescue centre during the school summer holidays.

1 Rick volunteered at the rescue centre because
   A he was worried about having nothing to do.
   B it would help him with his plans for the future.
   C there was little chance of him getting paid work.
2 The most interesting part of the work for Rick is
   A teaching the dogs through games.
   B meeting people who visit the centre.
   C learning from seeing the vet work.
3 What is the hardest part of the daily routine for Rick?
   A exercising the dogs
   B cleaning the sleeping areas
   C feeding some of the animals
4 What does Rick say about the other volunteers?
   A They all work every day.
   B There is a wide range in age.
   C He finds it hard to get on with them.
5 How does Rick feel about people leaving animals without a home?
   A He is surprised that they do it.
   B He can understand the reasons for it.
   C He gets angry with them for doing it.
6 What does Rick say about taking an animal to his own home?
   A He would like to, but he doesn't have enough space.
   B His parents have refused to have one.
   C He thinks he might be able to take a small animal.

Reading Part 6

For each question, write the correct answer.

Write one word in each gap.

A trip to the zoo

Recently, I went with my friend Tom on a trip to the zoo to celebrate his birthday and, while we were there, we saw a dolphin show. We watched the dolphins performing tricks for their trainers and I started wondering whether the dolphins **(1)** .... actually enjoying the tricks they had to do during the show.

When I came home, I looked **(2)** .... some information about dolphins living in zoos. I found an interesting article about dolphins which said they might actually enjoy playing games and doing tricks **(3)** .... they perform for the public. However, some dolphins have to keep performing in shows without having breaks. Unfortunately, **(4)** .... can make them very tired. And since food is used as a reward in the performance, dolphins may **(5)** .... get enough to eat if they don't do what the trainers want them to do.

Reading this information **(6)** .... me feel quite upset. I don't want to see another dolphin show ever again.

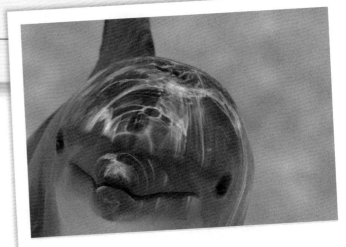

Writing Part 2

You see this announcement in an international English-language magazine.

> Articles wanted!
>
> **VOLUNTEERING**
>
> What volunteering job that you would like to do? What would it involve? Why would you like to do this particular type of volunteering?
>
> The best articles will be printed in our magazine.

Write your article in about 100 words.

Reading Part 2

For each question, choose the correct answer.

The young people below all want to find a website about animals. Opposite there are descriptions of eight animal websites.

Decide which website would be the most suitable for the following people.

1 Jodie is looking for information about animals affected by environmental problems. She also wants advice about looking after her pet parrot and would like some animal posters for her room.

2 Sebastian wants a website with a beginner's guide to drawing animals. He also wants to learn lots of facts about animals, especially sea animals, through playing games online.

3 Maya wants a website that teaches her new things about animals every day she visits it. She also wants to watch videos of baby animals and is interested to know how to become a vet.

4 Harry wants to research ways in which animals help people. He'd like to learn to take better photos of animals and visit an animal park to practise, without having to pay the full entrance price.

5 Eliana wants to read about rare animals. She also wants to spend her free time helping animals and is interested in taking part in a real research project.

Animal Websites

A Mad About Animals
This website has lists of animal hospitals looking for student volunteers. It also gives details of various studies into the number of different types of creatures found in gardens. People can get involved in these studies and upload their results. Whenever these include photos of very unusual creatures, experts add descriptions.

B Animal A–Z
Play different games every day on this website. There's a monthly free competition you can enter to find the most unusual animal photo. Last month's winner was two bears playing in a pond on a hot day. Winning photos are made into posters that people can buy from the webshop.

C Crazy Creatures
There are daily puzzles and quizzes, making this a popular website for students and teachers. If you've never been able to paint or draw animals, there are loads of easy-to-follow examples. The 'Animal Passport' pages contain all kinds of interesting information on unusual creatures living in our oceans.

D Planet Wildlife
Use this website's search engine to find zoos and other animal attractions near you, and download codes which give you discounts on tickets. The other great things about Planet Wildlife are the guide to animal photography and the brilliant articles about how certain animals have been helpful to humans for centuries.

E Animal Club
Draw, make videos or take photos of animals you see in your daily life, and post them on this website. They could be of your family pet or a rare bird, or even a baby animal you see at an animal park.

F World of Wildlife
This website has live action from inside an animal rescue centre where two pandas were recently born. It also has an 'Animal Facts' page that's updated daily. And the careers section includes details of training and qualifications needed to get jobs that involve looking after animals, from pets to zoo animals and animals in the wild.

G Animal Planet
This website contains sections written by vets on how to care for animals, birds and fish at home. There are interesting articles about research into the decrease in some animal populations because of climate change and pollution. You can also help animal charities by supporting the webshop, which has all kinds of animal gifts, including games, wall art and toys.

H Creature Corner
If you're looking for advanced lessons in drawing animals, Creature Corner is perfect. There are also cute pictures that people upload of their pets, from baby rabbits to enormous horses, and the online shop's particularly good for books and posters about whales and dolphins.

We're off!

Grammar

First & second conditional

1 Choose the correct word to complete these sentences.

1 If you get up early tomorrow morning, I *'ll* / *'d* cook you breakfast.
2 If you don't do any revision, you *won't* / *wouldn't* pass the exam on Friday.
3 If I had more money, I *'ll* / *'d* buy a new skateboard.
4 If you could go on a trip anywhere in the world, where *will* / *would* you go?
5 I'm not sure yet, but, if there's enough snow, we *may* / *would* go skiing next weekend.
6 If my dad had the choice between going somewhere by plane or by train, he *might* / *'d* always choose the train. He hates flying.
7 They *won't* / *wouldn't* have that beautiful new house if they hadn't won the lottery.
8 If I see him, I *will* / *would* tell him to call you, OK?

2 Complete these sentences with the verb in brackets in the first or second conditional.

1 I think I would be a bit frightened if I .... (have to) stay overnight at home alone.
2 If you .... (finish) all your homework by 7 p.m., you can play on your computer for a couple of hours.
3 She'll be upset if we .... (not get) tickets for the match.
4 If I .... (be) you, I wouldn't worry about it.
5 I would join the school orchestra if I .... (know) how to play a musical instrument.
6 If he .... (not get up) so late in the mornings, he wouldn't miss the school bus so often.
7 They wouldn't lose so many matches if they .... (practise) more.
8 Will you wash the car if I .... (pay) you to do it?

Vocabulary

1 Choose the correct word to complete this conversation between a girl and her father on the way to the airport.

Father: Oh no, not more red **(1)** *roundabouts* / *traffic lights*!
Girl: It's OK, Dad, we've got plenty of time.
Father: I'm not so sure. With that 30 kph speed limit on the **(2)** *motorway* / *platform* after that accident, we're late now.
Girl: Dad, my flight doesn't leave for another two hours, and we're nearly at the **(3)** *station* / *airport*!
Father: Right, well, you have already **(4)** *taken off* / *checked in*, haven't you?
Girl: Yes, and I've got the **(5)** *security* / *boarding* pass on my phone. It's really cool, I'm sitting in the first row – I'll be able to see the **(6)** *pilot* / *flight attendant* flying the plane!
Father: Great. Now you will remember to put your **(7)** *hand luggage* / *seat belt* on once you're sitting down, won't you? And what about your suitcase?
Girl: I've only got a small one, which I'm taking with me on the plane.
Father: Are you sure it's not too heavy?
Girl: Yes, Dad, I **(8)** *landed* / *weighed* it at home.
Father: Great! So when we get to the airport, you can go straight to **(9)** *security* / *station,* then. Will you be all right finding the **(10)** *gate* / *platform* after that?
Girl: Dad, I'm 16, I'll be fine! Please stop worrying. And I'll call you as soon as I **(11)** *take off* / *land* and have met Aunty Angela, I promise!

2 Complete this text message sent from someone on a boat trip with words in the box.

crowded   harbour   rough   waves

We're in a storm and the sea is very
(1) .... The (2) .... are about
three metres high. The boat is (3) ....
with people and lots of them are feeling seasick.
It's horrible! I can see the (4) .... in the
distance. I hope we get there soon!

2:34 ✓✓

✓ Exam tasks

Writing Part 2

You see this announcement on a travel website.

Articles wanted!

A FAVOURITE JOURNEY

What's the best journey you have ever been on?
Where did you go? Who were you with? Do you
think it's better to travel alone or with friends? Tell
us about the journey and why you enjoyed it.

We will publish the most interesting articles in our
magazine.

Write your article in about 100 words.

Listening Part 2

🔊 **09** For each question, choose the correct answer.

1 You will hear a girl telling her friend about
a train journey.
What was she surprised about?
A the price of the ticket
B the train leaving late
C the lack of available seats

2 You will hear a brother and sister talking about
taking holiday photos.
What do they agree on?
A They should take all their photos with their phone
camera.
B A camera is better than a phone for some types of
photos.
C People like taking photos of views when they're
on holiday.

3 You will hear two friends talking about a recent
school trip.
How did they both feel about it?
A disappointed that they didn't see more places
B pleased by the quality of all the accommodation
C surprised at being allowed to do things by
themselves

4 You will hear a girl talking about a coach journey
she has been on.
What might stop her travelling like this again?
A it makes her feel unwell
B the uncomfortable seats
C the length of the journey

5 You will hear a boy telling his friend about his
recent 'staycation'.
How did he feel after the holiday?
A disappointed that he hadn't been away from
home
B surprised by the amount of things to do locally
C pleased to be able to spend time with his family

6 You will hear a boy and girl talking about holidays.
The boy convinces the girl that
A holidays in hotels are the best.
B sleeping on the ground can be enjoyable.
C she would like a new type of camping.

Reading Part 3

For each question, choose the correct answer.

Trip to Paris

by Stephen Mitchell

When my mum told me she had to go to Paris for a business trip and suggested that I go with her, I have to admit I wasn't that keen on the idea at first. It's not that I wasn't interested in going to Paris, but I just didn't think it would be much fun with a parent! In the end, though, Mum managed to convince me that we would have a good time.

We live in London so we didn't have to fly. We took the Eurostar, which is a high-speed train that takes about two hours to get there. I thought that I might be a bit scared as the train travels through a 50-kilometre-long tunnel underneath the sea between England and France. But as we were travelling when it was already dark, I didn't even realise that we were in the tunnel until we were almost out of it.

Once we were in Paris, and apart from a couple of meetings on the first day, Mum was free the rest of the time. We did lots of sightseeing, including going to the Louvre Museum to see Leonardo da Vinci's painting called the *Mona Lisa*. I'm not usually a big fan of art galleries, but Mum persuaded me to go, and it wasn't as boring as I thought it was going to be. It was actually quite exciting to see such a famous painting in real life.

The highlight of the trip was when we visited the Eiffel Tower. This famous monument is 324 metres high and has three floors, which you can get to by lift, or you can walk up 669 steps to get to the first two floors! I wanted to go up to the top floor, but Mum refused. She's afraid of heights, and said she couldn't manage anything higher than the second floor. I was a bit disappointed – a friend had been all the way to the top and he'd told me that the view was amazing – but I tried not to show Mum that I minded. In any case, the view from the second floor was pretty spectacular.

---

1 In the first paragraph, how does Stephen feel about the trip to Paris?

A He wasn't clear why he had to go to Paris.

B He wasn't sure about going on this type of trip.

C He couldn't believe he was going to Paris.

D He was immediately interested about the trip.

2 How did Stephen feel before his journey on the Eurostar train to Paris?

A calm about going through a very long tunnel

B pleased that he didn't have to fly

C nervous about part of the journey

D curious to see what a high-speed train was like

3 The visit to the Louvre Museum

A confirmed Stephen's views about art galleries.

B was quite disappointing.

C was a better experience than he had expected.

D made him really want to visit other art galleries.

4 What happened when Stephen and his mother visited the Eiffel Tower?

A They were annoyed by how many stairs they had to climb.

B Stephen made an effort to hide his feelings from his mother.

C They were impressed with the view from the top floor.

D Stephen realised that he was scared of heights.

5 What would Stephen say to a friend about the trip?

A It wasn't all perfect, but I really enjoyed it.

B It was all fantastic. We did everything that I wanted to do.

C It wasn't great. I don't think I'll go on a business trip with Mum again!

D It was all right, although I didn't see anything really amazing.

Reading Part 4

You are going to read an article about holidays spent at home.

Five sentences have been removed from the text below.

For each question, choose the correct answer.

There are three extra sentences which you do not need to use.

HOLIDAYS AT HOME OR 'STAYCATIONS'

I love travelling. **(1)** .... There is nothing better than seeing new places, exploring different cultures, trying different food, just breathing different air. And there are so many places in the world that I want to see. **(2)** .... But that doesn't mean that you can't go on vacation (as they say in American English) at all. Instead, you can have a 'staycation'. This is a holiday spent in your home country or even in your own home.

A staycation could involve going away to a different part of your country or sleeping at home and going on day-trips to places near where you live. You won't get the chance to experience a completely different culture with a staycation, but it does have advantages, particularly if you go for the stay-at-home option. You don't have to decide which clothes to pack – and which to leave behind. **(3)** .... And you won't have expensive hotels to pay for as your accommodation will be free.

(4) .... We couldn't afford to go abroad on holiday so my dad suggested having a home-based staycation instead. He and my mum booked two weeks off work, just as if we were going away somewhere. Then we all made lists of things that we would like to do together locally. We knew that we couldn't do everything that everyone wanted to do, but the plan was to try and do at least three or four from each person's list.

I would say that, in general, our staycation was a success. There were some things that I wasn't mad about doing, like the 10-mile walk in the countryside that was on my mum's list, or the trip to the nearest big town to spend a whole day shopping – my sister's choice, of course! **(5)** .... Doing that with Mum and Dad, seeing them trying not to fall off, was really fun!

A   But we did quite a few things from my list, including horse-riding.
B   In fact, my friends joke I spend more time away than at home.
C   It's not possible to visit them all though, because of time and cost.
D   Last summer, for various reasons, we didn't have a lot of money.
E   There were several things on my staycation list.
F   This year, I am going to stay at home.
G   You will also avoid the stress of airports and delayed flights.
H   You won't be able to sleep in your own bed.

Vocabulary Extra

1 All about me!

1 Complete the words for schools.

1 a school for children aged between 11 and 18:
s _ c _ _ d _ r _

2 a school for children aged between 4 and 11:
p _ _ m a _ _

3 the part of a school for students aged between 16 and 18:
_ i _ t _ _ o r _

4 a school where students live and study:
_ o _ _ d _ n _

5 a school in the UK that is free to go to because the government provides the money for it:
_ t _ t _

6 in the UK, a school that you pay to go to; in the US, a school that is free to go to because the government pays for it:
_ u _ l _ _

7 another way of calling a school that you pay to go to: p _ _ v _ t _

8 a place where babies and young children are looked after without their parents:
_ _ r s _ _ y

2 Complete these sentences with a word from the box.

> certificate   curriculum
> degree   fields   qualifications

1 After three years studying at London University, she got a .... in biology.

2 When my grandfather was at school, Spanish wasn't part of the .... – French was the only foreign language that his school offered.

3 She's an expert in the .... of IT and engineering.

4 Have you got your .... to show that you attended the course?

5 You have to study a lot and to have good .... to get any type of job nowadays.

3 Match the sentence beginnings (1–5) with the correct ending (a–e).

1 I'm going to the library to do some research for our history project –

2 I love hanging out with friends at break time –

3 I find it quite hard to write essays –

4 We break up for the holidays on 8th July –

5 It's a pity that we don't go to the laboratory more often in science lessons –

a no school for two whole months!

b there are lots of books there that could be useful.

c I really enjoy doing experiments.

d I don't get the chance to see them much outside of school.

e I never know what to put in the conclusion.

2 Winning & losing

1 Match the words to make compound nouns for sports places and equipment.

> basketball boxing changing football golf
> hockey running track

1 .... room

2 .... track

3 .... pitch

4 .... net

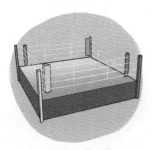 

5 .... ring

6 .... stick

7 .... course

8 .... suit

2 Look at these pictures. Write the correct letter next to each sport.

1 yoga ....   **5** jogging ....
2 horse-riding ....   **6** long jump ....
3 high jump ....   **7** boxing ....
4 ice hockey ....   **8** water skiing ....

3 Match the words for people in sport (1–6) with their definitions (a–f).

1 spectator   **4** referee
2 competitor   **5** champion
3 athlete   **6** instructor

a a person who takes part in track and field events, e.g. running
b a person who watches a sports event
c a person whose job is to teach people a practical skill
d the person who wins a competition
e the word for someone who takes part in a competition
f a person who is in charge of a sports game and who makes certain that players follow the rules

3 Let's shop!

1 Complete these words for clothes and accessories.

1 s _ _ _ _

2 b _ _ _ p _ _ _

3 p _ l _ _ v _ _

4 b _ t _ _ _

5 s _ _ p _ _ _ s

6 h _ _ _ _ _

7 s _ _ _ _

8 z _ _

2 Complete these sentences with the correct form of the verbs in the box.

fold up	not fit	go with	not match	suit	take

1 That jumper .... you. It's much too small.
2 Those socks .... – one's dark blue and one's black!
3 That jacket would .... you. You look good in blue.
4 Your feet are huge! What size shoes do you .... ?
5 Don't leave your clothes on the floor! .... them .... and put them on the chair.
6 These earrings .... perfectly .... my new dress.

3 Find ten words for things to wear or materials.

Z	I	Q	P	P	B	W	I	G	X	L	J	N	C	P
E	T	Z	P	N	E	S	G	K	C	O	F	L	O	P
S	B	S	O	H	R	I	Z	J	V	K	S	T	B	A
B	E	W	P	P	K	L	E	A	T	H	E	R	N	E
P	L	Z	L	B	G	K	E	Q	F	M	S	A	T	L
A	T	J	Y	O	P	J	V	M	E	K	X	I	C	I
O	F	A	J	A	C	K	E	T	U	Q	T	N	Q	M
W	I	M	E	D	L	H	D	A	G	C	N	E	U	S
A	K	Z	A	C	D	G	R	F	S	H	I	R	T	E
P	F	Y	N	B	R	M	G	C	C	Q	X	S	N	O
T	J	I	S	O	J	M	U	E	D	K	N	C	L	B
L	B	L	H	W	M	N	X	C	O	T	T	O	N	D
A	K	C	B	O	A	A	W	E	Q	X	G	J	E	H
N	S	T	R	O	U	S	E	R	S	I	R	T	W	P
M	J	R	X	L	K	K	P	O	V	X	A	A	Z	Y

....
....
....
....
....
....
....
....
....
....

4 Star quality

1 Match the types of film and TV programme in the box with their definitions.

chat show   comedy   documentary   drama
game show   horror   news   science fiction
soap opera   thriller

1 a film or a book with an exciting story, often about crime ....

2 a TV programme where an interviewer asks people questions about their lives ....

3 a film or TV programme that gives facts about a real situation ....

4 a funny film, one that makes you laugh ....

5 a TV programme where people play games to try to win prizes ....

6 a film or TV series with a serious story, usually with conflict between characters ....

7 a TV series about the daily lives of a group of people ....

8 a film or TV series with a story about life in the future or in other parts of the universe ....

9 a film made to shock or frighten people ....

10 the announcement of important events happening in the world ....

2 Complete these sentences with words from the box.

awful   brilliant   confusing   excellent   original
terrible   unusual   wonderful

We can use (1) ...., (2) .... and (3) .... to say that something is very good.

If something is (4) ...., it is difficult to understand.

(5) .... and (6) .... are used to say that something is very bad.

We use (7) .... to say that something is special and interesting because of not being the same as others.

We use (8) .... to say that something is different, not ordinary.

3 Complete the TV and film words and adjectives in these sentences.

1 The th _ _ _ l _ r we watched last night was so c _ _ f _ _ i _ _ – I didn't understand a thing.

2 I think the acting in most s _ _ _ o _ e _ _ _ is really bad, t _ r _ _ b _ _, in fact!

3 The d _ c _ m _ _ t _ _ _ about dolphins was so good, really _ x _ _ _ l _ _ t .

4 It's a very o _ _ g _ n _ _ d r _ m _ – I've never seen anything like it before.

5 I think that c _ _ _ sh _ _ is _w _ _ l – they never interview anyone interesting.

6 That new g _ m _ _ _ o _ is quite u _ u _ u _ _ . It has animals, not people, playing!

1 Put the letters in order to make cooking verbs.

1 keab ....

2 srota ....

3 urpo ....

4 glirl ....

5 gewih ....

6 tuc pu ....

7 clise ....

8 rubn ....

2 Complete these phrases with the words in the box.

> bananas biscuits bread chocolate jam milk
> soft drink soup tuna water

1 a carton of ....
2 a jar of ....
3 a tin of ....
4 a bar of ....
5 a bunch of ....
6 a packet of ....
7 a loaf of ....
8 a bowl of ....
9 a bottle of ....
10 a can of ....

3 Choose the correct words to complete these sentences.

1 Did you put chillies in this curry? It's much too *spicy / fatty* for me.
2 *Milky / Dairy* products such as cheese and yoghurt contain calcium, which is good for your bones.
3 She loves tea, but she doesn't really like coffee because it has such a *bitter / salty* taste.
4 That lasagne you made was absolutely *bland / delicious*. Can you give me the recipe?
5 Doctors say that we need to have a lot of *new / fresh* fruit and vegetables in our diet and that we should avoid *icy / frozen* and other types of processed food.
6 I love *barbecued / outdoor* food. There is nothing like a tasty burger cooked over a fire.
7 Don't eat those green bananas! They are not *mature / ripe* yet.
8 I love lemons, but my sister can't stand them. They are too *spicy / sour* for her.

6 My home

1 Match the words in the box to the photos.

| boiler | dishwasher | freezer | hob | kettle |
| microwave | oven | sink |

1 ....

2 ....

3 ....

4 ....

5 ....

6 ....

7 ....

8 ....

2 Look at the picture. Complete the words.

1 d...................   6 r...................
2 p...................   7 s...................
3 c..........of d..............   8 p...................
4 d...................   9 s...................
5 w...................

3 Match these words to their definitions.

| cashpoint | clinic | crossing | crossroads | gallery |
| garage | pavement | town hall |

1 a business that repairs or sells cars, and sometimes also sells fuel ....

2 a path by the side of a road that people walk on ....

3 a machine that you can get money from using a plastic card ....

4 a place where people can go across a road ....

5 a large building where local government is based ....

6 a room or building that is used for showing paintings and other art to the public ....

7 a place where two roads cross each other ....

8 a place where doctors or other medical workers treat people ....

7 In the wild

1 Complete these words for animals.

1 b _ _

2 m _ _ q _ _ t _

3 b _ _ _ e _ f _ _

4 f _ _ g

5 d _ _ p _ _ _

6 d _ n _ _ _

7 a _ _

8 g _ _ a _ _ e

9 d _ _ _

10 g _ _ t

2 Match the animal babies (1–5) with their parents (a–e).

1	lamb	**a**	cat
2	calf	**b**	chicken
3	kitten	**c**	cow
4	chick	**d**	horse
5	foal	**e**	sheep

3 Label the picture with the words in the box.

> bush   cave   cliff   hill   peak
> rock   stream

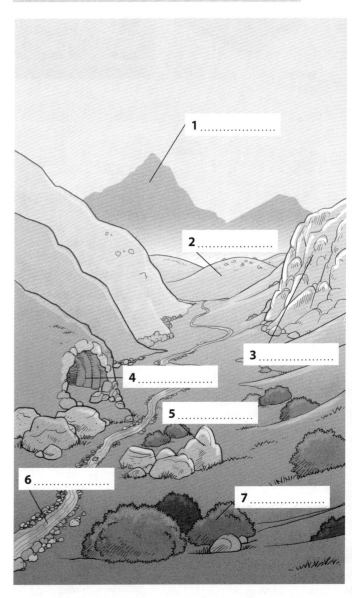

1 ....

2 ....

3 ....

4 ....

5 ....

6 ....

7 ....

We're off!

1 Match the words (a–h) with the correct definitions (1–8). Then complete the crossword.

a abroad   e duty-free
b border   f embassy
c customs   g currency
d exchange rate   h immigration

ACROSS

4 the money that is used in a particular country at a particular time
5 in or to a foreign country or countries
6 the place where travellers' bags are examined for illegal or taxable goods
7 the amount at which the money of one country can be changed for the money of another country
8 the group of people who represent their country in a foreign country and/or the building these people work in

DOWN

1 the process of examining your passport to make certain that you can be allowed to enter a country, or the place where this is done
2 the line that divides one country from another
3 items bought in special shops in airports, on ships, etc. on which you do not pay government tax

2 Complete these phrasal verbs in the sentences with the prepositions in the box.

| around   down   into   off x2   up |

1 We set .... late for the airport because my brother couldn't find his passport.
2 They showed .... about an hour late, but at least they came!
3 The first thing we need to do is to check .... the hotel so we can leave the luggage in the room.
4 The train broke .... because of a problem with the engine. I didn't get home until midnight!
5 There's no need to come to the station to see me .... We can say goodbye here.
6 I can't wait to look .... the city. It's my first time here.

3 Label the car with the words in the box.

| brakes   horn   mirror   steering wheel
tyre   wheel   windscreen   windscreen wipers |

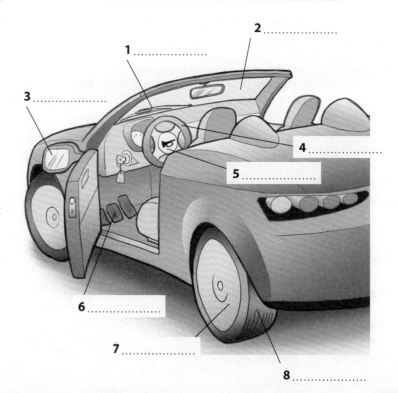

Workbook Audio scripts

🔊 **02** **Unit 1, Listening Part 2**

1 *You will hear a girl trying to persuade her friend to join a school drama club.*

Girl: Have you decided about the drama club yet, Seb? Are you going to join? We need more people for the summer show.

Boy: Hmm, I'm still thinking about it. I'm not sure it's my kind of thing. I mean, I've never done any acting before.

Girl: Well, I'm sure you'd be excellent at it. And, anyway, there are other ways you can help, like making costumes, lighting, doing the make-up, that sort of thing.

Boy: Oh really? I'd be interested in helping with the costumes. OK, I'll come and see what it's like. It's on Tuesdays, right?

2 *You will hear a girl talking to her brother about her new school uniform.*

Boy: I think it looks great. What do you think?

Girl: Well, I'd prefer to be wearing jeans, obviously! But it could be worse, I suppose.

Boy: The grey top looks good on you.

Girl: Thanks. I think the skirt is really nice. It's a much better style than the one I had at my last school.

Boy: That's true. Well, I thought it was fine, but I know you didn't like it. Now, what about the jacket? Aren't you going to put that on?

Girl: Right, yes, the jacket. That's the part of the uniform that I'm not so keen on!

3 *You will hear a boy telling his friend about a new teacher.*

Boy: Did I tell you that we've got a new teacher for maths?

Girl: No. What's she – or he – like?

Boy: She. Mrs Brown. She's really nice. And I like maths much better now.

Girl: That's good, because you didn't like it last term, did you?

Boy: No, but it's different with Mrs Brown. She explains everything really well, it's all clear, not like Mr Johnson. He was a nice person, but not a great teacher, and he gave us a lot of homework. Mrs Brown gives us just as much as he did, but I don't mind if I know how to do it!

4 *You will hear two classmates talking about a recent class project in which the girl got a high mark.*

Boy: I don't believe it! You got 90% in the biology project. How did you do it?

Girl: I can't believe it myself! I think I was lucky. But I did do a lot of research and planning. I went over everything that we had done in class. And I looked things up online when I wasn't sure about them.

Boy: I did all that, too, and I only got 60%!

Girl: When you did your research, did you make any notes?

Boy: No, I just read through everything and then wrote my project.

Girl: Ah, well, that's probably it. You can explain things better if you make good notes. You should try that next time.

5 *You will hear two classmates talking about their end-of-year trip.*

Girl: So what do you think about the trip?

Boy: It sounds great. I've always wanted to go to Italy. Just think of all those famous places that we're going to see!

Girl: I know. I've never been to Italy either. I can't wait to see Rome! And the food is going to be fantastic. I love pizza!

Boy: Who doesn't? The only part of the trip that I'm not so sure about is the project we have to do. Why do we have to work while we're there?

Girl: Oh, I think it's good. That way, we'll concentrate better on everything we're seeing.

6 *You will hear a girl telling her friend about a summer camp she went on.*

Boy: So how did it go at camp, Jo?

Girl: Well, when I arrived and saw that I had to sleep in a tent with five other girls, I thought I was going to hate it! But it was actually fun.

Boy: I bet! So you were doing German classes, weren't you?

Girl: That's what I signed up for, but not enough people wanted to do it, which was a pity as I was looking forward to them. So, I ended up doing lots of sport – not that that really bothered me.

🔊 **03** **Unit 2, Listening Part 3**

You will hear a woman called Susan Chapman telling a group of secondary school pupils about a sports centre.

Woman: Good morning. My name's Susan Chapman, I'm the manager of the Westfield Sports Centre, and I'm here today to tell you all about it.

Now, as some of you may know, the Centre was closed for a few months for improvements. We were hoping to be able to open again last July, but the work took longer than planned and we have only just opened now, in September. We were lucky as we got a grant from the local council, and, with this money, we were able to build a separate gym just for young people aged 12 to 16. And, now, as well as the old outdoor swimming pool for the summer, we have a new indoor one. It's 50 metres long and 25 metres wide, so perfect for serious swimmers to practise for competitions.

As well as the gym and the pool, we have a whole range of other sports and activities that you might be interested in. We have several team sports. In addition to basketball and football, which we've always had, we are now offering hockey on Saturday mornings. We also have individual sports. We're continuing our programme of classes for badminton, tennis and squash, and we've just opened a new one for gymnastics.

Oh, and I forgot to mention before that next to our tennis courts we now have a couple of courts for volleyball, a game which is becoming very popular.

And we have various dance and fitness classes for people of all ages, both young and old.

In case you're wondering how much it costs to sign up to Westfield, the good news is – it's not very much! To encourage young people to get fit, there is currently a 50% discount on membership for anyone under 18. And it's 25% for over 18s, so tell your parents!

Interviewer: Hello. Today, we have here 16-year-old Ella McHugh, who runs a business selling 'upcycled' products, which is a bit like *recycling*, but, rather than throwing things away, you make something old or used into a *new* object, often one of higher value. Ella, what gave you the idea for the business?

Ella: My dad told me about someone who'd invented a way to use plastic bottles as a sort of light bulb in places where people don't have electricity, and I thought that was really clever. So I started thinking about what materials I had around me that I could try and make into something useful.

Interviewer: And what was the first product that you made?

Ella: A bag out of some old jeans. I also made a lamp using an old bottle.

Interviewer: What did people think of the first products you made?

Ella: People weren't keen on the lamp, but they were positive about the bag and said I should make some more using other old clothes and try and sell them.

Interviewer: And how long ago did you start the business?

Ella: Well, I started making the bags around this time last year, but I didn't sell many. I needed to set up a website to be able to sell stuff, and it took me a few months to learn how to do that. So I'd say it was when it went online about six months ago that the business started properly.

Interviewer: And do you have any help making all the products that you sell?

Ella: I didn't at the beginning, and managed it alone for the first few months, but about a month ago, I asked a couple of friends if they wanted to help me. It's just too much work now for one person.

Interviewer: How do you feel about working with other people?

Ella: I'm really happy about it, because, although I'm the one who's in charge of the business, I'm not the only one responsible for having ideas and being creative, so it's less stressful for me!

Interviewer: And what do your parents think about you running a business?

Ella: At first, they were worried that it would take up all my time and that I wouldn't do my homework, and that my marks would go down. But they've seen that this hasn't happened, and, in fact, they think it's good that I'm learning about business and design, subjects that I don't do at school.

Interviewer: Thank you, Ella!

🔊 **05** Unit 4, Listening Part 1

1 *How is the girl going to celebrate her birthday?*

Boy: So have you decided what you're going to do for your birthday?

Girl: Well, I wanted to see a film, but there's not really anything interesting on.

Boy: Right. So what other options are there?

Girl: Mum said I could have a party at home, but only if I do all the tidying up afterwards.

Boy: That sounds like a lot of work! I know, what about going for lunch at that new Italian place?

Girl: That's a great idea! I'll start calling people.

2 *How old was the man when he started making films?*

Man: I made *The Lost Dog* when I was eleven, but that wasn't my first film. I remember going to the cinema with my parents when I was seven, and then really wanting a camera, but I didn't get one until my tenth birthday. And it was that summer, with my sister, that we made *The Family Secret* and posted it on YouTube.

3 *Which instrument does the girl still play?*

Man: So are you still playing the guitar, the drums *and* the violin? I don't know how you find the time to practise all of them.

Girl: Well, actually, Grandpa, I don't, that's the problem.

Man: So why don't you give one of them up?

Girl: I've given up two! I was going to give up the guitar and just concentrate on the drums and the violin. But, in the end, I realised that I loved playing it too much to stop, and I gave up the drums and violin instead!

4 *Who won the young film-maker competition?*

Girl: I thought the very tall boy with the fair hair was going to win. His film was really good. Amazing that someone so young could make a film like that. But the documentary by the girl with the long dark hair was excellent. I can see why they chose her as the winner. I felt sorry for that other boy, though, the short one with the long curly hair, but I wasn't surprised that his film lost.

5 *When do the girls decide to go to the concert?*

Girl 1: What days are the band playing?

Girl 2: The tour is from the eighteenth to the twenty-eighth of November, but they're only playing here on the twentieth, twenty-first and twenty-second.

Girl 1: Right, so what day of the week is the twentieth?

Girl 2: Hang on, I'll have a look on my phone. (*short pause*) Thursday.

Girl 1: OK, so that means the twenty-first is a Friday and the twenty-second a Saturday. I'd prefer to go on the Saturday night.

Girl 2: Yes, me too. Let's see if there are any tickets left for then.

6 *What did the woman buy her niece for her birthday?*

Man: So did you finally choose a present for your niece?

Woman: Yes, but it wasn't easy. I thought about earrings – she lost her favourite pair the other week, so I looked round all the shops but couldn't find any that were quite right. So then I thought about a T-shirt – I know she needs a red one to go with a new skirt that she's got. Then there was the book idea – she loves that series about the girl and the monkey, and a new book's just come out. But they had sold out at the bookshop. So I got her the T-shirt in the end.

7 *What time do the boys need to leave for the cinema?*

Boy 1: So what time do we need to get there?

Boy 2: Well, the film starts at 6 o'clock, but let's get there a bit before it starts, say at a quarter to six, so we can buy popcorn and stuff.

Boy 2: Yeah, OK. So we should leave here around 5 o'clock, then.

Boy 1: I don't think we need to leave until a quarter past five. It'll only take us half an hour to walk there.

Boy 2: OK.

🔊 **06** **Unit 5, Listening Part 3**

You will hear a teacher giving her students some information about a class trip to a farm.

Woman: Listen everyone! We're going on our class trip to a local farm tomorrow and I just wanted to give you a bit more information about it.

If you remember, for our trip to the TV studio last year, we had to leave really early, at about 7.30, because it was so far away. For this one, though, it's fairly near so we won't set off until 8.45, but please be here at 8.30 so I can check you're all here first.

The owners of the farm are providing lunch for everyone, so you don't need to worry about taking any food. However, it's worth bringing some money, as they have a small shop where you can buy souvenirs and sweets. There's lots to do at the farm, of course, and the owner has told me that after you've given the rabbits their morning meal, you'll be able to ride on the horses and even learn how to get milk from the goats.

They grow lots of fresh food on the farm to sell to local shops. You're actually going to be able to pick something delicious to take home with you. The strawberries won't be ready yet, unfortunately, but according to the farmer, there are plenty of beans ready for us to collect.

The farm also makes other things that it sells. They're hoping to start making ice cream in the near future, but we'll be able to have a taste of the cheese they produce. You'll also watch the jam being made, which should be really interesting.

If you or your parents want to find out more about the farm before we go, there's loads of information on their website at www.chalcotts.com. I'll spell that for you…it's C-H-A-L-C-O-double T-S dot com.

Does anyone have any questions?

🔊 **07** **Unit 6, Listening Part 1**

1 *Where is the girl moving to?*

Boy: So have your parents decided which place they're going to buy?

Elena: Well, they really liked the flat in the town centre, and I did, too, but then we thought that we would miss having space outside – a balcony just isn't the same as a garden.

Boy: So is it going to be that cottage, then, with the beautiful garden?

Elena: Well, we all loved that place. It was just a bit too far from things though. So, they've finally decided on the modern house with a garden and somewhere to keep the car.

2 *What job is the boy's mother doing now?*

Girl: Your mum owns a restaurant, doesn't she? Does that mean you don't see much of her if she has to work in the evenings?

Boy: She used to work most evenings, but she wanted to spend more time with my sister and me, so she decided to sell the restaurant and do something else and now she's teaching at a cookery school.

Girl: Hasn't she ever thought about writing a cookery book?

Boy: Oh yes. She plans to do that in the summer holidays.

3 *Where is the girl now?*

Girl: Mark, where are you? Didn't we arrange to meet at the library? I was waiting for ages there, but then thought maybe I'd got it wrong and you'd said the sports centre. Weren't you playing tennis before coming to meet me? So I went there, but they

said that you'd left about half an hour before. Anyway, I've just arrived at the department store in the centre of town. I remembered that I needed to get my cousin a birthday present. Call me when you get this message, OK?

4 *What will the weather be like in the north today?*

Woman: So what can we expect from the weather today? Well, starting in the north of the region, the sunshine and warm temperatures that we've been enjoying are now over, I'm sorry to say. They're being replaced by darker conditions including regular showers through the afternoon. Further south, things are looking better, which is good news for anyone planning a day out by the sea. You can expect sunshine and fairly warm temperatures, although it will be quite windy, so perhaps not a great day for a picnic on the beach.

5 *What does the girl still need for her room?*

Boy: So have you finished decorating your room yet?

Girl: Almost. My mum and I painted the walls last weekend – a really nice blue. And then there was the new furniture that we needed to buy – the bed and the desk – but we ordered all that a couple of weeks ago and it arrived yesterday, so that's all in place. The only thing we haven't done yet is put up the curtains. You could help with that, if you like?

6 *Which was the last place that they visited on the school trip?*

Boy: The plan was to go to the history museum first, but, with the coach breaking down, we were late arriving, so we had to go straight to the castle as we were booked for a visit there at 12 o'clock. That lasted about two hours, and we were all really hungry by then, so we took our packed lunches to the castle gardens, not to the picnic area by the river as planned. We then went to the museum later in the afternoon.

7 *Where did the boy stay on holiday?*

Girl: So, what was the hotel like? You said your parents had booked a really nice one.

Boy: They did, but something went wrong with the booking. When we arrived, they didn't have any rooms.

Girl: Oh no! What did you do?

Boy: The receptionist tried to find us another hotel, but there was nothing available. He tried looking for holiday apartments, too, but with no luck. All he could find was a cabin on a camp site! It was right next to the beach, though, so it wasn't so bad in the end.

🔊 **08** **Unit 7, Listening Part 4**

Interviewer: Today I'm talking to sixteen-year-old Rick Faraday who works as a volunteer at an animal rescue centre. Rick, can you tell us why you chose to volunteer at the centre?

Rick: I had three months of school holidays coming up, so I applied for a few jobs, and was waiting to hear back, when I heard they were looking for volunteers here. My dream is to become a vet, so I thought that this would be a great opportunity to get some experience of working with animals.

Interviewer: And what have you found the most interesting part of the work?

Rick: There are over 100 dogs here and we help train them by playing with them, and that's fun. We also have open days where people come to the centre if they're thinking of giving a home to an animal, and it's interesting talking to them. I also learn a lot from watching how sick animals are looked after. In fact, I can't think of anything better than that.

Interviewer: Is there anything about the work here that you find hard?

Rick: Most of the animals are shut in at night and we have to start the day by cleaning their pens, and that's not my favourite job! After that, we feed them, which I enjoy, although some of the dogs get very excited and jump up at me, which I don't like much. We also have to take the dogs out for a walk and some of them are really big, and it can be really difficult to control them, so that's the most challenging thing.

Interviewer: Tell us something about the other volunteers.

Rick: There are some other teenagers, although I think I'm probably the youngest, and there are some older people who have retired, but are still active and who come to help a couple of days a week. Everyone's really nice and friendly.

Interviewer: And how do you feel about animals being left without a home by people?

Rick: Well, *I* would never be able to do it, but I think that sometimes people just can't manage to look after an animal – maybe they've lost their job and can't afford the food – and feel they haven't got any other option. I think it's really sad.

Interviewer: Have you got any plans yourself to offer an animal from the centre a home?

Rick: Well, I'd love to, but we already have a dog, and our house isn't very big. I think, though, that I could possibly persuade my parents to let me get a cat. They don't take up much space, after all!

🔊 09 **Unit 8, Listening Part 2**

1 You will hear a girl telling her friend about a train journey.

Girl 1: How was the journey back from London, Ruth?

Girl 2: Not great! To start with, the ticket was really expensive, but Mum had said it was going to be, buying it at the last minute like I did. And then the train was late leaving, but that wasn't unusual. I mean, they always seem to run late. No, what I hadn't expected was that, after paying all that money for the ticket, there wouldn't be anywhere to sit down! I had to stand all the way to Brighton.

Girl 1: That's terrible!

2 You will hear a brother and sister talking about taking holiday photos.

Girl: You're not taking that old camera on holiday with us, are you, Dave?

Boy: Yes, I am! It takes really good photos.

Girl: Not as good as the ones I take on my phone. Look at these ones I took yesterday.

Boy: Hmm, they're not bad, but they're all close ups of you and your friends. What about when you want to take pictures of views, from a distance, like people often do on holiday?

Girl: Well, yeah, my phone's not so good for that, it's true. OK, you can take the camera!

3 You will hear two friends talking about a recent school trip.

Girl: It was a good trip, wasn't it?

Boy: Oh yes, it was brilliant, although it's a pity that the trip didn't include Venice.

Girl: Really? We went to five different cities in ten days! I think six would have been too many.

Boy: You're probably right. Anyway, what amazed me about it all was how the teachers let us go off on our own to explore places. I thought we'd have to be with them the whole time.

Girl: Yeah, I know what you mean. I wasn't expecting that either. I also thought the hotels were pretty good. Well, expect for that one in Rome.

Boy: Yeah, that was horrible. But the rest were OK.

4 You will hear a girl talking about a coach journey she has been on.

Boy: How was the journey down to your grandparents' place?

Girl: Oh, not great. I got really bored. I couldn't read a book, or use my smartphone, because doing so when I travel by road makes me travel sick. The funny thing is, it doesn't affect me on a train. It's such a pity because otherwise the bus was great. It was a bit longer than by train, but not by much and the ticket was cheaper. The bus even had lovely big seats, like nice soft armchairs. But the fact that I couldn't read or watch anything without feeling ill ruined the whole experience. Next time I go to see my grandparents, I think I will probably have to go by train, or even by plane!

5 You will hear a boy telling his friend about his recent 'staycation'.

Girl: How did your 'staycation' go, Alex? You weren't looking forward to it much.

Boy: I know. I'd been a bit upset that we couldn't go away as planned, but, with Grandpa ill …

Tom Yeah, I think your parents made the right decision. So was it boring staying at home?

Girl: We were hardly at home, actually. We went on lots of interesting day trips, to places I'd never been before. I didn't know there was so much stuff to do around here!

Girl: Great, you can show me some new places!

6 You will hear a boy and girl talking about holidays.

Girl: What do you think is the best kind of holiday?

Boy: Well, you can't really go wrong with a nice hotel somewhere, can you? But, personally, what I like best is camping.

Girl: Really? I'm not sure. I've never been, but sleeping in a tent on the hard ground can't be very comfortable.

Boy: Well, that might have been true in the past, but nowadays, you can go luxury camping – 'glamping' it's called – where you have proper beds, a bathroom, almost like a hotel.

Girl: Oh yes, that sounds more my thing!

Acknowledgements

The authors and publishers acknowledge the following sources of copyright material and are grateful for the permissions granted. While every effort has been made, it has not always been possible to identify the sources of all the material used, or to trace all copyright holders. If any omissions are brought to our notice, we will be happy to include the appropriate acknowledgements on reprinting and in the next update to the digital edition, as applicable.

Key: U = Unit

Photography

All the images are sourced from Getty Images.

U1: Raphye Alexius/Image Source; Jose Luis Pelaez Inc/Blend Images; KidStock/Blend Images; Science Photo Library/Getty Images Plus; Doug Menuez/The Image Bank; Marcus Lindstrom/E+; Robert Daly/OJO Images; xavierarnau/E+; U2: Alistair Berg/DigitalVision; Sirikorn Techatraibhop/EyeEm; shank_ali/E+; TuiPhotoengineer/iStock/Getty Images Plus; U3: Tetra Images; imagestock/E+; Issaurinko/iStock/Getty Images Plus; Chee Siong Teh/EyeEm; istanbulimage/E+; David Arky; dem10/E+; GaryAlvis/E+; Topic Images Inc.; Inga Linder-Kopiecka/EyeEm; U4: Sigrid Gombert/Cultura; Eric Audras/ONOKY; Image Source; U5: SSC/Taxi; Monty Rakusen/Cultura; Westend61; U6: Nino H. Photography/Moment; Glow Décor; gerenme/iStock/Getty Images Plus; Studio 504/Photodisc; Image Source; Howard Shooter/Dorling Kindersley; AlexLMX/iStock/Getty Images Plus; AndreyPopov/iStock/Getty Images Plus; Ng Sok Lian/EyeEm; U7: Hillary Kladke/Moment; mariuskasteckas/RooM; alejocock/Moment; Julian Schaldach/EyeEm; Tim Grist Photography/Moment; Westend61; Inigo Cia/Moment; David de la Iglesia Villar/Moment; IamDKB/Moment; Daisy-Daisy/iStock/Getty Images Plus; Ron Levine/DigitalVision; Vladimir Godnik; Rob Lewine; Hero Images; Michael Marsh/stocks photography; Joao Paulo Burini/Moment; Jacky Parker Photography; Gary Ombler/Dorling Kindersley; Gail Shotlander/Moment; Peter Muller/Cultura; Aukid Phumsirichat/EyeEm; Pierre-Yves Babelon/Moment; Ronald Leunis/EyeEm; Digital Zoo/DigitalVision; U8: Edmund Lowe Photography/Moment; © Philippe LEJEANVRE/Moment; Dieter Spannknebel/Stockbyte.

Front cover photography by William King/The Image Bank/Getty Images; Sir Francis Canker Photography/Moment/Getty Images; vladj55/iStock/Getty Images Plus/Getty Images; fitopardo.com/Moment/Getty Images; EnginKorkmaz/iStock Editorial/Getty Images Plus/Getty Images; Laurie Noble/DigitalVision/Getty Images; Pawel Toczynski/Photographer's Choice/Getty Images.

Illustration

Jo and Alina from KJA Agency; Giuliano Aloisi.